HO, HO F★★★ING HO!

ESSENTIAL YULETIDE READING

BY MARTIN BAXENDALE

ISBN O-9513542-7-2

Printed in Britain by Stoate & Bishop (Printers) Ltd,
Cheltenham & Gloucester: Typesetting by Alpha Studio,
The Old Convent, Beeches Green, Stroud, Glos.